David Stirling
Who Dares Wins

ANTON GILL

CONTENTS

WHO DARES WINS

ONE

Colonel Sir Archibald David Stirling, DSO, OBE, was born on 15 November 1915 and died on 4 November 1990. He was knighted in the last year of his life.

He was considered the most under-decorated soldier of the Second World War, since army protocol requires the presence of a senior officer as witness to any individual act of valour for a medal to be awarded, and the nature of Stirling's work was always that of 'deeds done in the dark'. His men, regardless of what rank he actually held, referred to him as 'Colonel David', and in general regarded him with a mixture of affection and respect. He was in his mid-twenties and a junior lieutenant in the Scots Guards when he formulated the idea of an undercover strike force designed to operate behind enemy lines, using the minimum number of men to effect the maximum amount of damage, instability and psychological disturbance to the enemy – the unit which soon became the Special Air Service. (Some argue that credit for its foundation should be shared with Welsh Guards Lieutenant Jock Lewes, and this is something which Stirling always acknowledged himself. Lewes was killed in action on 31 December 1941, ten days after his 28th birthday.)

Stirling was a man of many parts and many contradictions. He never married and he was cagey about his amours. He was good with people and could be as charming as he was persuasive; at the same time he shied away from personal commitment in his private life. As well as being a remarkable soldier and the moving spirit behind the foundation of the SAS, he was also a failed artist, a businessman, a patriot, at once a traditionalist and an innovator; both a political idealist and a political dabbler, an addicted gambler, and above all a man of action. A child of his time, his privileged economic niche and his class, and not the most reflective of men, he was never one to stand back, and some of his activities during the postwar years led many to suspect him of radical right-wing views. He did what he did because he thought it was the right thing to do. His weakness was that he seldom took other viewpoints into account. Yet he was never a racist, he had a strong sense of fairness, and if anything his somewhat naïve personal political stance leant (paradoxically) to the left – certainly his ideas for an African federation based on rule by merit, not by race or class, though they could never be realised, were ideologically sound.

He never, however, moved with the times and his view of the world remained essentially an Edwardian one, bounded by social confines which can be pinpointed: White's Club, the Clermont, the Guards regiments, the Conservative Party and the British aristocracy. 'The rich man in his castle, the poor man at his gate, God made them high and lowly, and ordered their estate' is a general approximation of his attitude, but it isn't wholly inaccurate. Although a maverick, it was in the waters of the British Establishment that he swam most easily. Ascetic when he chose to be, he was also a bon viveur who was more than a match for generous helpings of Famous Grouse and Sancerre; and he smoked good cigars in a stubby holder.

In the quarter-century since David Stirling's death, the world has undergone major political and social shifts. It's important to remember the historical, social and political context in which he lived.

He never trumped the triumph of his great wartime innovation. The SAS was a brilliant idea, conceived along sound business-practice lines (its cost-effectiveness was perfect), as well as military ones, at a time when most generals were still thinking in terms of the nineteenth-century set-piece battle. The Second World War saw much military innovation – von Stauffenberg's treatise on paratroop warfare will be remembered as an example – and the techniques of the SAS are a cornerstone of what modern boots-on-the-ground warfare now is. But despite Stirling's ardour, enthusiasm and stubbornness in seeing it to fruition, elements of his character ensured that it was not – under his stewardship – an unequivocal success.

The appraisal just given is an overview. To be fair to Stirling, one must give him the chance to reveal himself as his story unfolds, in his mixture of driven energy, complexity, and disingenuously engaging simplicity of manner.

TWO

A monument to David Stirling stands midway between Doune and Dunblane, north of his ancestral home of Keir, and the town of Stirling. The 2.74m high statue by Angela Conner, unveiled in 2002, shows a duffel-coated Stirling bracing himself against a strong wind – the wind of the Scottish moorland, of the north African desert in which he operated, of the opposition which he so often found himself up against. The statue is larger than life-size, but Stirling himself stood an impressive 1.98m tall. However his size and presence, which are well suggested by the bronze, belie a delicate childhood.

Stirling was born into an ancient Scottish aristocratic family at a time when the First World War had just put paid to the relative tranquillity and stability (at least for the ruling classes) of the Victorian and succeeding Edwardian ages. The massive estate, which had been in the family since the mid-fifteenth century, gained its present house in the 1760s, while the family's extensive holdings in Jamaica enabled them to make successive improvements both to the house, grounds and farms in the succeeding years, notably under the aegis of Stirling's formidable grandfather, the 9th baronet, Sir William Stirling-Maxwell, MP for Perthshire, Chancellor of Glasgow University, bibliographer, cattle-breeder and enthusiastic and progressive art collector. His older son, Sir John Stirling-Maxwell, succeeded to the estate of Pollok. His younger son, Brigadier-General Archibald Stirling of Keir, married a daughter of Lord Lovat, Margaret Fraser, who was fourteen years his junior, in 1910. The couple had six children, of whom Archibald David was the third son. His older brothers William and Peter were both to play significant roles in his life; his younger brother, Hugh, was killed in action in Libya in 1941 a month before his 24th birthday. He had two sisters; Margaret, one year his senior, was his close childhood friend within the family.

Keir is no longer in the possession of the Stirlings. In 1975, the heir, David's oldest brother William, sold it, together with 15,000 acres of the estate, to Mahdi al-Tajir, a UAE businessman, for £2million. Twenty years later, the furniture, heirlooms and much of the art collection were sold for a further £1.5million.

But the Keir of David Stirling's boyhood was a typical patrician upper-class household. Though beatings were virtually unknown – the Brigadier-General detested violence, but ill-manners and any damage to his cherished gardens would result in a severe lecture – the children were taught to keep their feelings reined in. If anything, it was Stirling's mother who held the greater sway over the children. Stirling recalled, 'I had a great respect for her … A respect which was tinged with awe. You see she always seemed to know what to do and what was in my mind and this could be quite, quite awesome. She never actually frightened me, but I cannot remember ever disobeying her directly. I often did, of course, when we were separated by distance but never in her presence.' His sense of duty to his mother had obliged him not to cry as a young boy after a painful tooth extraction – his mother hadn't wished him to discourage two younger siblings, Hugh and Irene, whose turn it was next.

Stirling's father was 8 years old when his own father died. He was not a professional soldier but had joined the colours in response to wartime call. He'd also married late – in his 43rd year. He'd inherited his father's love of the arts, was more than anything a scholar and a poet – by instinct and by education, but he took the duties his birth had imposed upon him seriously. Both parents, however, were inclined to be protective of David. Though full of pluck and mischief, he was a small, delicate child. A bad accident increased their concern. Holidaying on the Isle of Mull, David had been bitten on the leg by an adder, and the resulting swelling was so severe that the local doctor had advised amputation. Only his mother's forceful intervention prevented this.

He made a full recovery, but he was beset by other trials early in life. He was slow to develop physically, and his frustration with this resulted in fits of sulking which could last for hours, although an appeal to his sense of humour, used most effectively by his brother Hugh, could break the mood. Another early disadvantage left a permanent mark: until the age of four, when it was recognised and corrected, a malformation of the tongue made him unable to articulate words correctly, and he had to communicate via his sister Margaret, who alone was able to understand him fully. Thereafter, Stirling was always at pains to be extremely concise both in spoken and written communications, and nothing irked him more than to find people slow on the uptake. Another effect may have been his tendency either to use malapropisms or to invert the syllables in a word ('halycon' for 'halcyon', for example), though often he did this consciously for comic effect. Humour, not necessarily subtle, was another hallmark of his character.

The Stirlings were an old Catholic family and the chapel at Keir, designed by David's father in 1912 with mosaics by the young Russian artist Boris Anrep, was in regular use. David grew up to be a practising Christian, and he never wavered in his belief in Christianity, though in boyhood he would (with his brother Peter) alleviate the boredom of Mass by seeing which of them could swing the censer right round in a circle without being noticed. Being a generally wild child, the family dispatched him to the Catholic public school to which it traditionally sent its sons, Ampleforth, at the relatively early age of eight-

and-a-half, and it was there that he made his first career 'contact' – Freddie de Guingand, though it must have been a tenuous one. Guingand was fifteen years David's senior, at the time briefly attached to the school's Officer Training Corps.

Stirling was not a model pupil. He was never, ever, one to conform to a disciplined regime. He enjoyed art and languages but did not excel particularly academically, as he wasn't interested. Likewise, though a good sportsman, team games were not for him, and he preferred to take himself off for long solitary rambles in the North Yorkshire countryside, stalking animals and setting his imagination free. He was introduced to hunting early, and many of its skills would serve him well when he applied them to the field of battle. Lacking discipline and playing truant, he was often punished; but he wasn't expelled. His time at Ampleforth was in any case often interrupted by bouts of ill-health. The adder-bite took a year out of his school-life, and later, in his early teens, he caught typhoid, which meant another long spell away from school. During these periods he was placed in the hands of a private tutor, and this method of education may actually have suited him better, though he remained wayward. As a child, he had terrified family and staff alike at home by rushing around at breakneck speed on his bike, especially after dark, and the constant thirst for action which he seems to have been born with manifested itself for the first time in the form of an organised raid when he was at home during one of his enforced absences from school.

The raid involved food. David's appetite was large, and that was a good thing because it helped build up the frail physique he had begun with. One evening, finding his early schoolroom supper at Keir especially unsatisfying, he decided to descend on the kitchens. His own rooms were at the opposite end of the house and he had to make the journey undetected via a series of staircases and long corridors. He managed to reach the kitchen without incident and found it deserted but he lingered too long in collecting some pudding to add to the cold meats, bread and pickles he'd already looted, and was discovered by the cook, who gave chase as he fled. The chase was joined by his mother's maid and the butler, all maintaining a profound silence so as not to disturb the Brigadier-General and his wife who were entertaining guests. David made it back to his room and locked the door against his pursuers in the nick of time; and apparently the incident was not reported.

If this was an early indication of his ability to plan and carry through a simple hit-and-run raid, he also demonstrated an early ability to manipulate people and circumstances to his advantage in a skilful ad-hoc manner. Though this story may be apocryphal, it's certainly in character. During a stay at the family's hunting-lodge, which enjoyed similarly resplendent gardens to Keir's, one of the keepers persuaded the family cook to have a ride on a pony. It was her first ride ever, and she lost control of the animal, which rushed wildly through the flowerbeds and kicked up the lawn before throwing the cook, who wasn't hurt, though she was very flustered. There was great hilarity, but it subsided fast as the Brigadier-General loomed, surveying the wreckage of his garden with a face of thunder.

When he asked who'd been responsible for the prank, David owned up. He got a severe dressing-down, but thereafter he also got extra portions at meals from the grateful cook.

Recovering from his various ailments, and eating heartily, Stirling at last began to round out and grow. His confidence never seems to have been in much question, though he remained daunted by his mother; and with his new-found strength he was at last able to take part in country pursuits alongside his brothers. He rode, trekked the hills, stalked and shot deer, and fished. He'd apply some of the techniques he learned on the moors to his later military activities.

A shadow fell during his 16th year, when his father died; but his mother remained a directing force in his life, and by the time he went up to Trinity College, Cambridge, he had not only reached his unusual height, towering over most of his peers, but had also developed a rangy, tough physique. His interests remained firmly with the arts, and fine arts in particular. As far as sport was concerned, the proximity of Cambridge to Newmarket led to an attraction to racing, and it was a natural step from that to gambling, to which he remained addicted for a great part of his life. No-one should be surprised at that, since Stirling's temperament was one which fed on risk. He was a fast and reckless driver and the victim of many self-inflicted accidents, often ending up with broken bones and long spells in hospital. By his own admission, during his lifetime, he wrote off at least five cars.

He'd also begun to learn consciously how to use his charm to get people to do what he wanted them to. As for university politics, he remembered that 'I was encountering young Communists for the first time and took great pleasure in opposing their stuffy, second-hand arguments…' It's tempting to think that he crossed the bows of some of the members of the Cambridge Five: Maclean and Cairncross were only a couple of years older than he was.

Whatever else he did at Cambridge, he partied hard and he didn't study much. He was bidden to his moral tutor's rooms, read out a list of twenty-three offences, and asked to select three on whose grounds he was to be sent down. He chose the three which he felt would cause least offence to his mother, packed his bags, and went home to Keir.

THREE

Looking at the dominating interests of his father and grandfather, and his own youthful forays in that direction, it isn't surprising that David now decided that his career lay in the arts – and not indirectly. He would go to Paris and he would study to be an artist. This was the first prompting of a romantic nature and it's interesting to reflect on what his life might have been like if he'd been able to develop that career.

Paris in the mid-1930s was a delightful, louche and slightly dangerous place for an artist to live. Stirling took to it like a duck to water, and, at least outwardly, shed his background and embraced a bohemian one. He also played down his relative

wealth. It was here that he had his first really
serious brushes with women; but he was never one
to be tied down. At the slightest suggestion of
permanence, he made his excuses and left.

Talking to his fellow students he both
broadened his horizons and respected, in his way,
the idea that, after all, socialism did have a point.
He didn't, however, for a moment relinquish the
conviction that his own class had merits and its
own part to play in society. He dedicated himself
to his work, and, when he was in a good mood,
turned out respectable floral still-lifes; darker
moods produced sinister abstracts. He experienced
the depression and frustration all creative people
feel when what they really want to express eludes
them, and this he recognised in and shared with his
new friends. He'd invent gambling winnings to
justify the occasional generous use of his money to
entertain them, and in his desire to fit in he dressed
the part. 'I loved those evenings,' he remembered.
'They were full of fervent speeches, chest-beating,
and the pomposity of youngsters who thought they
were being totally original. In fact their views were
distinctly second-hand, bolstered by the booze and
all the more plastic for that. I suppose I was a little
false and plastic myself. I spent some of my brasso
[his word for money] on buying clothes which I

imagined allowed me to blend – corduroys which I deliberately made dirty and the regulation beret and scarf. No matter how cold it was I made my protest along with the others and never, never wore an overcoat…'

It was not to last. He couldn't make his art work, however hard he struggled, and at last his tutor, the eminent artist André Lhote, told him that, though there was no doubting his creative power, 'I lacked absolutely the basic drawing expertise, and in his opinion I would never achieve it.' Stirling remembered this blow as being the most bitter disappointment of his life.

This was perhaps the one major failure he would ever encounter, or at least which hurt him; and the experience made him all the more determined to succeed, to express his originality elsewhere – though the unfinished business, the battle which could never be won, haunted his memory. He went home, was able to return to Cambridge, joined an Edinburgh architectural practice when he came down, which wasn't a success, and at the end of the 1930s found himself at an impasse, looking enviously at his siblings, who appeared to have their careers happily mapped out.

He still gambled, and he still had a thirst for risk-taking. He was big and strong and loved a challenge. He was without the need to earn money. So he decided on a new, grandiose project. There had been three British expeditions to climb Mount Everest in the early 1920s and they had caught his imagination. The intrepid George Mallory, present on all three, had died in his last attempt in 1924. Stirling wanted to take up the challenge. He would be the first man to reach the summit of Sagarmatha.

To this end, he embarked on a rigorous training programme, financed by his mother, first in the Swiss Alps, and latterly in the Rockies. He also enlisted in the Scots Guards Supplementary Reserve, believing that 'this might help in some obscure way', and more specifically hoping to brush up his navigational skills and toughen himself up still further. His father had been in the Scots Guards, so it seemed the natural regiment to choose. In the event, he loathed the endless drilling and what he regarded as totally useless tactical exercises at the Pirbright Camp near Aldershot in Surrey. At least the place was within stabbing distance of the fleshpots of London.

In the event, too, the Rockies project was delayed because Stirling arrived en route to them at New York at the end of 1938, and the 23-year-old, taking a suite at the Pierre, no less, found the city too alluring to leave. He had flings with women, but once again withdrew if things looked as if they were getting serious, and he gambled his money away, resorting to his indulgent mother to refinance him, or soft-soaping the family bank manager over the phone into granting him an overdraft. When the charms of New York palled, he took himself off to British Colombia and worked as a cowboy for a while.

Everest wasn't getting any closer, but he did make it to the Rockies at last, which he explored seriously, and steeped himself in the culture of the Native American nations he encountered, as they were people with whom he keenly identified. But he also gambled in Las Vegas, travelled in Texas, and continued his American meanderings until they were interrupted by the news, on 1 September 1939, that Britain was once again at war with Germany. He wired home for more precise information and got an immediate reply from his mother in which she said: 'RETURN HOME IMMEDIATELY BY THE CHEAPEST POSSIBLE MEANS'.

Stirling promptly caught the next available flight.

FOUR

Later in life, Stirling became interested in education and its importance in the creation of responsible adults, and about a year before he died he talked more candidly than usual about his own schooldays, and his experiences and difficulties with both religion and love. In the small hours one morning (he was always a night-owl) he told his friend, former comrade-in-arms, and biographer Alan Hoe: 'School was something of a misery for me. I was a failure at most subjects except perhaps history – no, not so much a failure as uninterested. I could have been better at sports but it was all marred by a tremendous anxiety neurosis … I was Master of Beagles for a while and during that period I just ran and ran; it was a mindless physical exercise I could get quite lost in. At Cambridge I was totally vague though I did have periods of great enjoyment – usually non-academic. I was quite convinced that I was a great artist and even though I was bad at drawing I was deeply involved with picture composition. Even after André Lhote gave me the bad news that I was not going to make it as an artist, I remained a constant doodler.'

'Doodler' can be taken as modesty. Stirling's upbringing taught him to suppress inner demons; disappointment and a sense of failure being two of them. As for the commitment of marriage, Stirling told Hoe that his reason for avoiding it was 'Fear, Spike [Hoe's nickname], sheer fear. Seriously, I don't think I have ever lived the sort of life which I could ask a woman to share … As a youth sex caused me no end of problems and I was in a total mess over it … My religion placed impossible standards on me without any understanding or sympathy. Every sexual thought and action was a sin – why was it a sin and why was it never explained properly? It is a part of growing up and simply cannot be bottled up as I tried to do. The bottling up of emotions, mainly guilt, left me in a real mess which I don't think I got out of until I made the decision to climb Everest … My first real sexual encounter was as a schoolboy, and with a woman I might say, and within minutes I went through intense feelings of pride and, I suppose, wonderment, followed by an even more intense guilt, hence all the running. Maybe I was hoping to escape it through sheer exhaustion. Certainly in Africa during the war (which brings another set of pressure) I never hesitated to check out the headquarter equipment; since then, "I've taken my fun where I found it" – Kipling, wasn't it?'

Stirling's mother died in August 1972, a couple of months after her 91st birthday. Late in life, he looked back on that time, during another late-night conversation. By that time, he had managed, apparently, to overcome his gambling addiction, but he remained preoccupied with his shortcomings: 'I've always said that I've been subjected to four pressures in life. The first was my mother. I loved her dearly and had the most enormous respect for her, but she was always asking what I was going to do with my life. I didn't know, of course; the more I thought about it the less I was able to see anything clearly. She was right, I had to make up my mind, but a combination of that and the totally confused, guilt-ridden years of puberty exerted an awful pressure. It seemed unbearable then.

'Having made up my mind that I would paint, the disappointment of my lack of talent left me feeling pretty useless, and surrounded by quite brilliant brothers and sisters. This was a second pressure … I was very worried when I was summoned to Scotland because my mother was dying – I was terrified of being there. I stopped for a drink on the way, not far short of the house, in fact. A little bit of me may have been hoping I'd be too late – I still don't know. In fact I did arrive before she died and I think she gave me a bit of a telling-off for being tardy.'

Together with the pressures of his mother, his early inability to find his path, and his sense of failure, was the fear of intimate personal commitment and its concomitant, loneliness. As we'll see, Stirling spent the latter part of the war as a PoW, and that experience affected his psyche further. 'Overall, despite one's companions in misfortune, I experienced a great loneliness. Planning a break-out or setting one's mind to problems as we did is only a temporary escape. Reality returns and with it guilt, claustrophobia, secret yearnings and the singular uselessness of one's own situation. Since the prison days I've never been at ease in a crowd and I've always been happiest in wide open spaces. It's not just a physical thing – it's mental as well; paper commitments, contracts, they've all given me the "jitterbuggers" – I don't like to be tied. Bonds of any sort are a pressure I find very difficult to bear.'

Family and friends he could cope with, as long as they knew where the limits lay (though he even baulked at the responsibilities of a godfather). For the rest, his instinctive and inevitable reaction was to seek both solace and relief in action.

In late 1939, the stage was set which would provide him with ample opportunity for that.

FIVE

It wasn't going to happen overnight. The first port of call after arriving back home was Pirbright again, and the – to Stirling – mindless routines and disciplines of a military training camp were all but unbearable. His individuality and his imagination were too well developed for him to feel anything but caged in such an environment. He'd learnt much about real tactics and fieldcraft from his hunting, shooting and fishing days in Scotland; he had the wit to see how they could be applied in warfare, and he was eager to be off to put his ideas to the test. Unfortunately his confidence and his sense of his own position in life did not endear him to his instructors; he didn't help matters by demonstrating his contempt for the outmoded techniques he felt he was being taught. He left, still in the rank of Guardsman, branded as an 'irresponsible and unremarkable soldier'.

However, he was in luck as far as career prospects were concerned. As he was an expert skier – a product of his days in Switzerland – he was soon able to join a battalion of the Scots Guards designated to be part of a task-force created to assist Finland in its fight against Russia early in 1940. Stirling, with his expertise, was promoted instructor-sergeant. But the task-force never saw the light of day, and Stirling returned to base, passing much of his leisure time at White's, the old-established gentlemen's club in St James's, then as now one of the bastions of the British Establishment, and one of the best places for making like-minded contacts. It was here that he had another stroke of luck, as it was in the club's corridors that he got wind of Colonel Robert Laycock's plans to raise the first unit of Commandos from the Guards regiments. The Commandos were organised for special service in June 1940, immediately following the evacuation of the British Expeditionary Force from Dunkirk. Winston Churchill had stipulated that the force 'must be prepared with specially-trained troops of the hunter class who can develop a reign of terror down the enemy coast'. By autumn, 1940, 2,000 men had volunteered. Among the volunteers was Stirling, who joined as a newly-commissioned subaltern.

Now among crack troops, he took his new training sessions far more seriously, and he enjoyed being put to the test in Scottish field exercises which involved unarmed combat and survival techniques. New fighting methods were developed and discussed, not simply imposed. Nevertheless, Stirling had his reservations about them, as his own ideas began to dawn. 'We plunged around the glens like one of the thundering herds of cattle I'd helped drive in America. It seemed wrong. There we were, being taught the art of silent killing and the like, signalling our presence to all and sundry as we ground forward in unwieldy groups of twenty or more.' In the meantime, his already-impressive physique hardened further, while his deceptively gentle nature and his well-deployed charm earned him affection, respect, and loyalty.

In February 1941 the Guards Commando to which Stirling was attached became part of Layforce. Layforce, named after its commander, Colonel Laycock, was formed of a number of commando units and designated for service in the Middle Eastern theatre of the war. The Guards Commando became 8 Commando of this group. Layforce's job was to conduct raiding operations on the enemy's lines of communications. Serving alongside Stirling was another volunteer from the White's network, Churchill's son, Randolph. They were brought together by their shared love of gambling – Randolph had heard of David's reputation from their mutual acquaintance and fellow officer Evelyn Waugh, who was at the time with the Royal Marines. As they prepared for action, Stirling was able to use this to his advantage: '[Randolph] was a likeable chap, but dear me he could talk. Not a bad thing, as he could never concentrate on his cards long enough to win; I really did stock up the sporran at his expense.' Gambling was a source of excitement to Stirling, but it also exercised his fascination for balancing risk and calculation.

March 1941 saw Layforce in Suez, preparing an assault on Rhodes, but after the German's successful conquest of Crete, and the German Army's subsequent commanding presence in Greece and the Western Desert, Middle East Headquarters retrenched. Layforce no longer seemed to have a role, and its highly-trained men were relocated into regular army units. Stirling found himself in Cairo, awaiting his own relocation, as MEHQ decided what to do with what remained of the group.

Fortunately, his elder brother Peter was attached to the British Embassy at the time, and had a flat in the Garden Quarter of the city. This provided David with a welcome bolthole from where he could indulge whenever he could in the delights Cairo had to offer – notably drinking, gambling and (up to a point) womanising. From a friendly nurse at the Scottish Hospital he learned the trick of taking a few deep breaths of pure oxygen from a bottle to alleviate instantly the effects of a hangover, but this necessitated frequent trips to the hospital, which were noticed; and when during a military night exercise thought to be the prelude to an operation he scratched his eye on a thorn branch, which meant genuine hospitalisation, his records were examined and an investigation was set in motion to determine whether or not he was a malingerer who might qualify for court martial on the grounds of cowardice.

Unaware of this, Stirling was discharged and returned to his base, where he now met a man who was to play a crucial role in the next stage of his career. Captain John – 'Jock' – Lewes of the Welsh

Guards had acquired a batch of about fifty parachutes originally destined for use in India as no parachuting role had been planned for troops in Africa. Nevertheless, Lewes had got permission from Laycock to use them, together with a bunch of half-a-dozen volunteers, in an experimental capacity. Stirling, bored with the lack of action, volunteered too, and took part in a trial drop from an old Vickers Valentia transport biplane not properly adapted for the purpose.

The drop used the static-line system. The static-line is a cord which is attached at one end to the aircraft and at the other to the parachute pack. As the jumper leaves the aircraft and falls into space, the line pulls the pack free of the parachute. The pack and the line are hauled back into the aircraft and the jumper, whose weight and the upward force of the wind cause the parachute canopy to open, starts to make his descent. When the inexperienced David made his first jump, his chute caught on the Valentia's tailplane and ripped before pulling free. He therefore fell towards earth far too fast, and although he had had basic training for impact (hitting the ground after a normal drop using a World War Two parachute had the same impact as jumping off a 15-foot wall and needs to be compensated for by going into a roll), all David could do was shut his eyes and hunch up. The resulting contusion of his back temporarily robbed him of the use of his legs and put him back in the Scottish Hospital. However, his undoubted bravery and commitment led to the inquiry into his previous behaviour being dropped, and the experience, plus the time in hospital, gave him time to think, and to crystallise a few ideas of his own. Commando raids had been from the sea, and needed enough men to set up a beachhead defence as well as an attack force. The naval backup required also made the operation cumbersome. Stirling knew that a few men could be dropped near a target, go in and reconnoitre, do their job, then vanish into the desert to a pre-arranged rendezvous with land-transport to take them back to base. That transport might be provided by the Long Range Desert Group. The LRDG was a small, highly-specialised, recently-formed unit for in-depth desert reconnaissance, and used to operating far behind enemy lines. Its volunteer members were all experienced in desert terrain and navigation and would provide essential backup. The retreat from the attack might be long and arduous, but the attack itself could have the element of total surprise, require few men, and be an ideal deployment for airfields, parked planes, fuel dumps and the like.

He discussed the idea with Lewes. It certainly had appeal, and it had been used in the past to great effect. As long ago as the Seven Years' War, Major Robert Rogers had developed a Corps of light infantry which was used in scouting and special operations to such great effect that Rogers' Rangers had become the chief reconnaissance arm of the British Army by the end of the 1750s. Lewes recalled them now, and was enthusiastic. But he was also pessimistic about Stirling's chances of getting anywhere with it. If a similar force were to be created now, it would have to have the imprimatur of the highest military authority. Despite his family cachet, which might be as much a hindrance as a help, Stirling was a pretty-much untried junior lieutenant, and he was only 25 years old.

But he was never one to turn his back on a challenge – in one way, it was all part of the game – and he was aware of the advantage of always going straight to the top with any idea of importance. Otherwise it would run the very obvious risk of being discussed or re-edited into oblivion, or just chucked into a pending file or – worse – a wastepaper-basket. The first step was to codify his aims in writing. This he did, in a lengthy document addressed to the Commander-in-Chief, Middle East Forces – then General Claude Auchinleck. Its title was A SPECIAL SERVICE UNIT, and it not only outlined its size and mode of operation, but also projections and concise plans for the new unit's use as part of the British Army's planned offensive for November 1941. It was by no means impeccable – in fact it was a work-in-progress; but for there to be any further progress, there had to be backing.

Stirling decided that the best way to cut to the chase was to deliver his memorandum in person.

SIX

This wasn't going to be easy. Stirling was back on his feet after his accident, but still using crutches, and he couldn't walk more than fifty metres – with difficulty – without them.

He took a taxi to MEHQ and once there observed the entry procedure at the gate and reconnoitred the perimeter fences of the compound. He had no pass and no appointment, so he took a chance on bluffing his way in. The guard was unimpressed with the excuse that he'd forgotten his pass, and for all his charm and powers of persuasion, Stirling was unable to sway him. He limped away on his crutches until he came to a gap he'd previously noticed where the fence post didn't quite come up flush to the guardhouse wall. There was a large tree conveniently close to the entrance and there David lurked until he saw that the sentries were sufficiently distracted by the traffic of people coming in and out. Dropping his crutches, he limped the few metres to the gap, squeezed through, and hurriedly joined a group of officials making their way towards the main building.

He'd got as far as the steps to the main entrance before he was noticed. Ignoring the shouts of the sentries, he staggered up the steps and into the building, disregarding the agonising pain in his legs. Once inside, he hurried as best he could along a corridor until he came to a door marked ADJUTANT-GENERAL. That seemed like a hopeful place to start and he went straight in, to be confronted by an immaculately-dressed and extremely outraged major whose face seemed familiar, though he couldn't place it. His first job was to pacify the major, so that he wouldn't raise the alarm, but once he'd introduced himself he realised that he'd put himself in hotter water than ever, for the major turned out to be one of the tutors Stirling had so studiously ignored during his first stint at Pirbright. Beating a hasty retreat, and knowing that now the hue and cry would be truly raised against him, he set off blindly through the maze of corridors until he came to another door, this time marked DCGS. The Deputy Chief of the General Staff. Well, in for a penny … He pushed the door open and went in, mollifying words already on his lips and the tension of the moment at least helping him forget the pain in his by now buckling legs.

Luckily, General Neil Ritchie was more biddable than the major. He allowed Stirling to gasp out his reason for being there, and then, noticing how much pain the young officer was in, he asked David to sit down, before accepting the memorandum and reading it. He took his time, reading it through twice, and then looked up and said, 'There may be some merit in this   '

The ball was set in motion. Now all he had to do was keep it rolling. The first difficulty presented itself when Ritchie introduced Stirling to the Adjutant-General branch officer who'd be responsible for assisting Stirling through the army's administration and personnel services. This officer turned out to be none other than the offended major, and his section would turn out to be a more-or-less permanent thorn in Stirling's side.

When Ritchie referred the idea to the Commander-in-Chief, however, Auchinleck was inclined to listen. At that time in the war, the German Army's Afrika Korps was in the ascendant under Generalleutnant Erwin Rommel. (It was Rommel who gave Stirling the sobriquet *Gespenstmajor* – the Phantom Major – which was later picked up by the British Press, and stuck.) Auchinleck was under pressure from Churchill to strike back, but he was husbanding his resources and was keen on the idea of such a plan as Stirling's, which demanded little equipment and few men, and looked as if, if it worked, it could indeed cause the maximum amount of damage with the minimum amount of outlay – and if it didn't, little would have been gambled. Stirling was soon bidden to a high-level meeting, promoted to Captain, and given the go-ahead to recruit six officers and up to sixty men, of whom a large proportion could be senior NCOs, and therefore experienced soldiers. He had a ready-made recruiting pool to hand in the remnant of Layforce, so all that remained was to choose a name for the unit.

It happened that Brigadier Dudley Clarke, responsible for disinformation and deception in the Middle East theatre, had set up a bogus paratroop brigade to unsettle the Afrika Korps. Dummies were parachuted close to PoW compounds, and mock-up gliders were set up on runways, to deceive German Intelligence. This imaginary group even had a name: the First Special Air Service Brigade. Clarke suggested that Stirling adopt the core of this name for his new unit, which became formally known as L Detachment, SAS Brigade. David insisted that 'L' stood for 'Learner'.

This was mid-July, 1941. There was a lot to do before the November offensive.

SEVEN

Stirling was very aware that he'd be recruiting seasoned fighters and, in the light of his own relatively slim combat experience, he was wary of being their commander. His confidence, however, didn't waver. The first person he wanted to get on board was Jock Lewes. However, 'I think Jock wanted to be sure that if we got the thing working, I was going to stay with it and also tackle the enormous problems at MEHQ which he possibly foresaw more clearly than me. It's true that he still wasn't in full agreement with the small unit concept but I reckon he thought he could talk me out of the bits he didn't like. He just didn't want to get involved if it was going to be a short-term flight of fancy. Jock was a serious sort of chap, he could be very short on humour and I suppose I'd come across to him in the past as a bit of a good-time Charlie. You wouldn't, for instance, find Jock catching a quick drink in Cairo, or taking a flutter at the racecourse.'

Lewes did join, after some persuasion, and when he did he brought four experienced men with him, a huge and significant contribution. They were Sergeants Pat Riley and Jim Almonds, and Privates Lilley and Blakeney. These were quickly joined by Stirling's own old platoon sergeant, Ernie Bond, and Reg Seekings, 'Benny' Bennett, Johnny Cooper, Bob Tait, Dave Kershaw, Jimmy Brough, 'Whacker' Evans and 'Tubby' Trenfield. After this core had been formed, volunteers came forward at a good rate, and once the basic unit had been formed, the men made their way to their allocated base camp at Kabrit, about 150 kilometres east of Cairo, on the edge of the Great Bitter Lake.

There they found little to welcome them, for the antipathy Stirling had unconsciously aroused in the AG branch major had borne its first fruit. They'd been given three old tents and an ancient three-ton lorry. Stirling was heartened by the fact that this discovery didn't faze his men at all, and he decided to turn the situation to his advantage by organising their first raid. Not far away lay a compound with an extremely well-equipped New Zealand camp, whose occupants had more than they needed and no supply problems at all. Without giving a direct order, Stirling just happened to mention this to his men, together with the fact that on a certain night the New Zealanders would be out on exercise. Guards were only posted on the compound perimeter. Anything that went missing – if all went well – would be put down to thieving locals, and be written off.

The compound containing the NZ camp also comprised units of British, Australian and Indian troops. Driving their old three-tonner, the men of L Detachment, led by its Senior NCOs, bluffed their way past the guards at the gate and drove through the compound unchallenged until they reached the NZ quarters. They doused the lorry's lights, armed themselves with torches, and started to take an orderly stock of the deserted camp. They had about five hours to select, load and carry off everything they considered necessary, together with a few luxuries as well. So as not to draw any attention to themselves, they used their torches sparingly; and their eyes soon became accustomed to the dark as they rummaged through what turned out to be a veritable Aladdin's cave. Necessities included tents – they carried off a good dozen small ones – hurricane lamps, washbasins, mirrors, latrine tents, chairs, tables, kitchen equipment, crockery, glasses and cutlery. The recreation room provided the luxuries: a small piano, and the contents of a well-stocked bar.

They loaded their truck up the gunnels and were about to leave when, at the last minute, a Military Policeman turned up. During the night various incurious inhabitants of the compound had drifted past, but now there was a real possibility of danger. However, the MP was only after a light for his cigarette, and either his suspicions weren't aroused or he chose to let them lie. In any case, the L Detachment raiding party was able to make a safe getaway.

Once their camp, now fully-equipped, had been properly established, Stirling made it clear that the unit was not to be regarded as beyond the bonds of army discipline just because it was new and based on a much less formal concept of warfare. They were still soldiers, not buccaneers, even thought their methods might be those of buccaneers. Auchinleck and Ritchie might be behind them, but Stirling was acutely aware of the unfriendly eyes of MEHQ on them. L detachment would give

MEHQ no cause to criticise or block. Furthermore, he forbade any indiscreet talk in the bars of Cairo or Alexandria; there was to be no brawling, and in general standards both of dress and comportment were to be maintained to a standard as high as that of any Guards regiment. Stirling put Lewes in charge of training – in which he himself took part alongside his men. One of the reasons he commanded such loyalty was that he was always hands-on. He did everything he expected his men to do; he was personally involved in almost every raid except that first one on the NZ camp.

But initially other duties demanded that he be away from Kabrit. He had recruited four more officers after Lewes, but he needed more, and to that end he returned to Cairo. One officer already on board, the 20-year-old Lieutenant Eoin McGonigal of the Royal Ulster Rifles, had mentioned a friend of his, a fellow Ulsterman called Blair Mayne, nicknamed Paddy, who McGonigal thought would make a great addition to the team. The only problem was that Mayne was currently in prison awaiting court-martial for striking his commanding officer, Geoffrey Keyes, a highly-regarded 24-year-old lieutenant-colonel who had already been awarded the Military Cross and the Croix-de-Guerre.

Mayne's drinking, temper and unpredictability were notorious, but he was also tough, fearless and intelligent – three qualities which Stirling had in his sights. But over time Mayne would test Stirling's leadership qualities.

Eleven months Stirling's senior and born into a landowning family, Paddy Mayne had excelled both as a boxer and as a rugby player, winning six caps while playing for Ireland as a lock forward in the 1930s. But on tour in South Africa he'd gained a reputation for trashing hotel rooms, and on one occasion he helped a convict he'd befriended break out of prison. He joined the Royal Ulster Rifles in 1940 and first saw action as a lieutenant with 11 Commando, successfully commanding his men during the Litani River operation in Lebanon against Vichy French forces. He became one of the army's most highly decorated soldiers, though the fact that he was never awarded the VC was still being debated as late as 2005. His men, while they admired his courage, remained wary of him, especially during the broodingly quiet moods which followed his drinking bouts. He survived the war, but died at the wheel of his Riley Roadster, after a night's drinking, in Newtownards, County Down, in 1955. He was as tall as Stirling, but heavier set, and, Stirling remembered, 'spoke in that gentle Ulster brogue which could charm the faeries'.

Stirling pulled strings to interview him, and eventually got his agreement to join L Detachment – if Stirling could get him out of the court-martial, which would have ended Mayne's military career at a stroke. Mayne wanted to shake on the deal but Stirling refused to do so until he'd exacted Mayne's promise that he would be one commanding officer whom Mayne would never hit, impressing on this loose cannon that discipline was paramount. He then pulled more strings, and the charges were dropped, as Keyes was a generous enough man to recognise the qualities in Mayne which counterbalanced his waywardness.

Once the new unit was up to strength, training started immediately. This was to be an elite force working in small interconnected units, or patrols. All ranks trained to the same degree, and a sense of mutual reliance and dependency regardless of rank was instilled. As most of their work was to be done at night, emphasis was placed on developing radio, weapons, first-aid, explosives and navigational skills in the dark. Endurance and physical toughness were of prime importance, and anyone who fell below the overall standard would be dropped without question from the force. The only outsiders would be experts brought in because of their particular skills, or to train group members in those skills. Each patrol would have a first-aid expert, a driver/mechanic, a navigator and an explosives specialist.

Everyone had to master parachuting as this was the initially-chosen method of going in. This was hard as the only parachute training school was at Ringway in England, and the help it offered was so rudimentary and unaccommodating that Stirling and his officers, principally the highly methodical Lewes, had to devise their own ways and means – a tough job, as they didn't even have a plane at their disposal, and had to practice by jumping off speeding lorries. As for endurance in the desert, Lewes formulated training by testing ideas out on himself: he would set out on long night-time desert marches, carrying a specifically-weighted pack and a specifically-measured amount of water, walking to a point at which he calculated he had used up half his reserves of strength, and then returning, calculating the kilometres he had covered and the time it had taken and using these as a model for training.

All this time Stirling was also dealing with administrative logistics and fighting battle after battle with the bureaucrats of MEHQ to get L

Detachment properly up and running. The clock was ticking and the time of the November offensive fast approaching. He was away from Kabrit a lot, but 'I was totally confident in Jock and Paddy and the others and it seemed to me that I just had to get the formalised establishment right at MEHQ. All those shits were against me; they sparked only when Ritchie took a personal hand, and I couldn't keep bothering him. I also thought it would be unfair to burden the others with the problems. I didn't want to give anyone the slightest reason to doubt that what they were working for was anything other than a reality.' Stirling's own indiscreet and sometimes tactless manner didn't help, but he was learning as he went along.

Stirling was also learning about the loneliness of leadership. With him away, the men were associating more and more closely with Mayne and Lewes as their commanders, and Stirling was also aware that his reputation as a lightweight – a man-about-Cairo rather than a serious soldier – might undermine his authority. All the work he was doing away from Kabrit might not measure up in the men's eyes to the hard physical stuff they were doing.

Stirling soon had a chance to prove his mettle. He'd finally got MEHQ to give him a Bristol

Bombay (the plane which was replacing the old Valentia) for real parachute training. The Bombay had been fitted for parachuting with proper anchor- and static-lines. Stirling took his place in the first round of jumps, which were successful. But soon afterwards two chutes failed to open and the jumpers were killed. The fault was traced to a defective link on the line which – Stirling soon discovered – Ringway was aware of, having had a similar experience there only shortly before. He was furious, had the fault rectified, and made the first jump after that himself, before allowing anyone else to do so.

Another technical difficulty to be overcome in developing this new form of warfare was the type of explosive to be used. As things stood, a typical fit-for-purpose incendiary bomb weighed well over two kilograms and took ten minutes to set up. Carrying enough such bombs to destroy a large number of planes on an enemy airfield, or damage ships in a harbour, or wipe out ammunition dumps, would be impossible as the combined weight would be too great. An alternative had to be found, and Jock Lewes – MEHQ having once again failed to rise to the occasion – set out to find it.

The Lewes Bomb has now passed into legend, but its invention was quick and almost accidental.

It was dangerous work, but Lewes calculated his chances. He organised a consignment of plastic explosive – then a new invention – and mixed it with thermite (a composition of metal powder, fuel and metal oxide which can create brief bursts of high temperature in a small area when ignited by heat) and oil, and the result was malleable and could be cut into blocks weighing about 500 grams each. Lightweight and adaptable, easy and quick to fix and detonate, it was the perfect weapon for the nascent SAS.

Stirling set up a full operational rehearsal which was observed by an RAF Group Captain who was to report to Ritchie on L detachment's chances of success. Everything, including the parachute drop, went without a hitch, but the Group Captain was still sceptical of their chances of actually infiltrating an enemy airfield and carrying out a successful raid, including getaway.

Stirling contained his impatience. 'It is a matter of common knowledge that aerodromes are always badly guarded, including our own,' he said in his usual deceptively mild manner. He then bet the man £10 that his men could get onto the RAF airfield at Heliopolis at any time they chose, place labels on the planes in lieu of bombs, and make a clean escape. The RAF could even warn the airfield guards that they were coming. 'We'll be there around the end of the month.' It was now October. The November deadline loomed, and Stirling didn't want to have to cut through any more blinkered thinking – there wasn't time; this would be not only a good test for his men, but an undeniable demonstration of their efficacy. There was another advantage: he'd already sensed that the constant training was beginning to pall, and the men were restless. They needed to see action or they'd go off the boil.

Heliopolis was about 130 kilometres from Kabrit, and they decided to launch the raid directly from their base camp – crossing that amount of desert with only two litres of water per man, carrying packs full of stones to simulate the weight of the bombs and other equipment they'd be carrying in a real operation, would test resilience to the full. Moving only after dark, they reached Heliopolis in the middle of the fourth night. Some of the men were by then suffering from hallucinations and reality-detachment owing to water deprivation, but now, with the airfield in sight, everyone focused.

Despite the advance warnings they'd given, they were able to approach the perimeter wire and cut through it unchallenged. Paddy Mayne's section went in and placed about fifty labels on planes – at the end of the exercise, some planes, targeted by the other patrols which were arriving at timed intervals, carried three or four labels each. Once the labels had been placed, the patrols lingered for a while, just to confirm that they'd been unchallenged. Then they made their way to the central guard-post to confirm the raid. Not only was their arrival unexpected, they were taken at first for Italian deserters or at best enemy troops surrendering. After five days in the desert they were so dishevelled and unkempt that they hardly looked like soldiers at all. But they'd won the bet and vindicated themselves beyond question, to the embarrassment and consternation of the RAF and MEHQ.

All Stirling's struggles with inflexible authority, and all his tenacity, had paid off. And he'd gained the well-deserved respect of his men, as their unquestioned commander. Mayne and Lewes played vital parts, but it was Stirling who had worked himself to near-exhaustion, not only in physical training with L Detachment, but in the greater and at times totally disheartening fight for what he believed would be a winning card in Africa, and beyond.

Auchinleck's offensive – Operation Crusader, designed initially to relieve Rommel's siege of Tobruk – was scheduled for 18 November 1941, three days after Stirling's 26th birthday.

EIGHT

The success of the dummy raid on Heliopolis excited a good deal of attention for the first real one. The attention made Stirling uneasy, especially as the weather forecast for the night of the operation – 16/17 November – was bad, with winds of up to thirty knots. This time the detachment would parachute in, linking up with a Long Range Desert Group patrol sent to pick them up at a designated rendezvous after the operation. Winds just above fifteen knots were known to be enough to scatter paratroopers; winds even higher than that could be dangerous to the point of injury and death.

Intelligence knew that there were five forward German airfields in the region of Gazala, on the coast west of Tobruk, and nearby Tamini. The plan was to send in patrols of about a dozen men to each airfield, and disable or destroy as many planes as possible. On account of the weather, General Staff were inclined to call the raid off. On a moonless night they'd have problems enough in regrouping, but with winds that high the risk of injury was enormous, let alone the problem of regrouping.

But it was left to Stirling to make the final decision. 'It seemed to me that we had to take the risk but I didn't exert any other influence. Mayne and Lewes immediately went along with my suggestion and the others quickly followed.'

The task was going to be incredibly difficult from the word go, as the planes taking them over the drop zone would have difficulty identifying it, even if they managed to see the marker flares which had been dropped in advance. Furthermore, supplies and equipment were to be dropped separately, in canisters. These too would be blown off course by the wind, and by the time they'd been located and collected – if they could be – and the men united, most of the darkness they needed for cover would be used up.

But Stirling had to balance these considerations against his relationship with MEHQ, which he was sure would be glad of any excuse to use a cancellation as a reason for diminishing L Detachment's potential; and there was the question of his men's morale: they needed real action and a sense of purpose now. Early in the morning of the operation, he had Mass said for the Catholics in his force, before the flight to the forward base. On 16 November at 19:30 five Bristol Bombays took off from there carrying one patrol in each, led by Stirling, Mayne, Lewes, McGonigal, and Lt. Charles Bonington. (Bonington deserves a brief mention: he was born in Britain; his father was German, changing his name from Bönig to Bonington. Charles Bonington was the father of British mountaineer Chris Bonington.)

Contrary to the forecasts, the night was fine and clear, but as they approached Gazala and Tamini cloud built up and the wind rose dramatically, throwing the planes around and forcing the pilots to descend to get a visible fix on their position. Worse, the planes got separated and Bonington's (Number 4 Flight) attracted German anti-aircraft fire, which hit the port engine and smashed the instrument panel, forcing it to crash-land. Accounts vary, but it seems there was a skirmish with German troops on the ground, when the co-pilot was killed. The rest were taken prisoner.

Stirling's own patrol managed to make the drop despite the fact that the marker flares put down earlier by Bomber Command were obscured by cloud; but as they parachuted down they were so buffeted by the wind that they were scattered, and when Stirling hit the ground, he did so with such force that he was knocked out for a good two minutes. In the meantime he was dragged at speed across a terrain of gravel and small rocks. A sandstorm was raging, but miraculously the patrol reunited, though it took two hours for them to do so. Most had various degrees of injury, two men seriously, one with a broken wrist, the other with a broken arm. They also failed to locate their equipment, except for a handful of blankets and a dozen Lewes bombs, without their fuses. The only weapons they carried were their revolvers, and they had a day's supply of food. They failed to locate their missing man, and there was nothing left to be done but rendezvous with the LRDG on the Trig-al-Abdh caravan route which crossed the desert to the south west. But the desert surrounded them as day dawned was vast and featureless. They knew their rough position and calculated they had about seventy kilometres to cover – if they set out in the right direction. There followed a nightmare thirty-six hours only relieved by a heavy rainfall which ensured a supply of water. At last, after Stirling had been tested to the limit as a desert navigator, they reached the rendezvous.

Slowly the events of the disastrous sortie were pieced together, as the remainder of the other surviving patrols were reunited. Mayne had lost two men; Lewes had brought back eight of his patrol. There was of course no news of Bonington's; and McGonigal's was never heard of again. The mission had been a failure, with a loss of forty of the original sixty-two man group.

There were comrades to be mourned and there were also hard lessons to be learned. Parachuting in no longer seemed a viable option. The way forward – if there was going to be one – was going to have to be with the collaboration of the LRDG.

The mission may not have achieved its aim, but Stirling knew that he'd been able to come close to the Germans and get away before they'd had time to react. The principle worked. He lost no time in discussing possibilities for the future with the LRDG people who escorted the survivors of his group back to LRDG's base at Siwa Oasis, an ancient desert settlement on the northern edge of the Great Sand Sea. Knowing that those against him at MEHQ would delight in his failure, and that Auchinleck and Ritchie would be too busy to give him much time, he determined not to return to Cairo until he'd found a means of proving the worth of the SAS beyond a doubt. He decided not even to return to Kabrit personally, and to cut off contact until he'd planned a raid which the rump of his force – the remaining twenty-two men – could carry out by themselves. This raid would be against an airfield, since the Luftwaffe was the biggest stumbling-block Auchinleck was encountering.

To do this, Stirling needed supplies, and he needed the support of the LRDG.

Meanwhile the British were advancing; as they did so, some further members of SAS teams were recovered. Empty bunks and tents at Kabrit were reclaimed, and the mood lifted. Stirling sent Lewes back there with instructions to pick up and return with as much equipment as he could manage, and in the meantime he found Lt.-Colonel Guy Prendergast of the LRDG, the unit's new commander and a fellow Scot, completely amenable to the idea of collaboration between his force and Stirling's. There was a lot the two unconventional and buccaneering units had in common.

In the meantime, too, Neil Ritchie had been made commander of the 8th Army and summoned Stirling to its HQ, not far from Siwa. To Stirling's relief, Ritchie merely questioned him about what he'd observed of Axis traffic on the coast road on the coast road, and offered his sympathy over the abortive first mission. The SAS clearly had breathing space.

The next bit of good fortune was an introduction to Brigadier Denys Reid, who was occupying Jalo Oasis, about 300 kilometres west of Siwa, on the north-western corner of the Great Sand Sea. Reid was able to meet Stirling's supply concerns, and the SAS regrouped at Jalo, agreeably far from army officialdom, and conveniently close to Stirling's desired field of operations, as it was only about 300 kilometres south of the coast.

Here a plan quickly evolved. Reid's squadron was ordered to link up with another British force outside Agedabia, near the coast about 100 kilometres south of Benghazi and at the western end of Trig-al-Abdh. However, if Reid made a move from Jalo, he'd be threatened fatally by the Luftwaffe bases at Agedabia itself, at Sirte, and at Agheila. Staggered raids were planned on all three airfields in advance of Reid's projected arrival on 22 December. Stirling and Mayne would hit Sirte and Lewes would hit Agheila on the night of 14/15 December; a third officer, Lt. Bill Fraser, would attack Agedabia on the night of 20/21, to cover the last leg of Reid's march. Each patrol would be made up of only a handful of men, there were only twenty-two of them after all, and the LRDG would take them to the targets.

Stirling and Mayne were spotted by an Italian Caproni Ca. 309 Ghibli reconnaissance aircraft before they'd left the LRDG and decided to split up as the alarm would clearly have been raised. Mayne went on to Tamet airfield, a little further west of Sirte, and Stirling remained with only one man, Sergeant Jimmy Brough, an old comrade in arms, to deal with Sirte. The two men advanced on foot, careful to draw no attention to themselves.

On arrival at Sirte they saw the airfield packed with Caproni ground-attack planes but held off planting their bombs as they needed to synchronise their attack with Mayne's. Unfortunately they disturbed a couple of off-duty Italian guards who panicked and raised the alarm, though Stirling and Brough were able to make their escape. But as they waited for things to die down, they noticed that the fighters were taking off and soon the airfield was empty. They later discovered that the planes had merely relocated to Tamet, and that was good news for the SAS, as soon afterwards they saw flashes of flame in the air to the west and heard the bombs going off – Mayne's raid on Tamet had clearly succeeded.

They made their own way back to make a perfect rendezvous with their LRDG vehicle and returned to Jalo. Mayne's patrol got there the following day. The attack on Tamet had gone without a hitch – twenty four planes destroyed and no casualties. Mayne had climbed up to the cockpit of the last plane and smashed it up with his bare hands, as they'd run out of bombs. But he'd also machine-gunned a hut full of enemy soldiers before the bombs were laid. That had raised the alarm, and they'd only completed the operation and got away in the nick of time.

Jock Lewes returned from Agheila to report a partial success. The airfield had been empty, but he'd managed to blow up a large number of vehicles. Fraser, however, had bypassed the sentries at Agedabia with his small patrol of three men, and destroyed thirty-seven planes. There had been no Detachment casualties whatsoever.

Far from returning to Kabrit on the back of this success, Stirling decided to remain in place and build on it by launching another raid as soon as possible. With his usual deceptive diffidence, he suggested rather than ordered this new attack, telling Fraser, who'd only recently got back, that he might care to go along and have a crack at the airfield designated 'Marble Arch', which was 'only' 300 kilometres away. The other targets were Sirte and Tamet again, with another at Nofilia thrown in, which Lewes was responsible for. (Stirling's ability to get the best out of his men by implying that they were all in it together, and that it all might be a bit of fun, showed his good psychological insight and got the best out of his men without ever compromising his authority.)

Mayne once again 'lit a bonfire' at Tamet, destroying another twenty-seven Italian planes which had only arrived within the past twenty-four hours. At Sirte Stirling was disappointed to be confronted by an empty airfield, though his patrol was able to wreak havoc on enemy transport vehicles on the coast road. But the relative success was tempered by tragedy. Fraser's group missed its rendezvous with LRDG and only got back to Jalo, where they arrived more dead than alive, after an eight-day trek through the desert. Lewes and his men had destroyed two aircraft at Nofilia, but on their way home they were strafed by enemy aircraft and Lewes was mortally wounded. He died on 31 December.

NINE

Back at the SAS base at Kabrit, Stirling took stock. In Lewes he'd lost his right-hand-man, the person he was looking to for dealing with recruitment, training and administration. These were things he'd have to shoulder, with the help of Mayne, though he knew Mayne wasn't cut out for those kind of tasks.

On the plus side, though the recent successes hadn't been as spectacular as he'd hoped, they were undeniable successes and more than compensated for the disaster of the first raid; and the working relationship with LRDG gave him a much better and more reliable raid-approach method than parachuting. What he needed to do now, and urgently, was recruit more men. Almost as soon as he'd washed and shaved and donned a fresh uniform, but leaving the beard which he'd grown in action, he set off for Cairo and MEHQ. The British offensive was going well – it looked as if Benghazi would soon be taken. If so, Rommel would be forced to use Bouerat, about 400 kilometres west along the coast from Agheila, to harbour his supplies. Bouerat therefore seemed a good next target for the SAS. And a harbour suited Stirling for other reasons: he didn't want his unit to be viewed as a strike force only to be used on airfields: it was its versatility he wanted to demonstrate now.

The beard was a bit of a statement, and aroused expected comment, but his request for an appointment with Auchinleck was quickly acknowledged and before too long he found himself being complimented on his beard and congratulated on his raids by the Commander-in-Chief. Auchinleck then asked him what his plans were.

This took Stirling aback but of course he was extremely pleased – he'd expected to have to fight in order to make his next move. He outlined his plans for Bouerat. Auchinleck agreed to them, accepted the need for absolute security, and therefore also agreed that Stirling should henceforward report directly to him. The C-in-C was also perfectly happy with the arrangement Stirling had made with LRDG. A time-frame for the Bouerat raid was set: the night of 24 January was moonless, and L Detachment could be back at Jalo by the 10th. Stirling then requested an additional fifteen men. Auchinleck told him he'd better recruit an extra forty, as well as six new officers, and promoted him Major.

This was a brilliant imprimatur, but time was tight and there were still the 'fossilised shits' – his hidebound enemies in MEHQ – to deal with. Auchinleck had other things on his mind than the SAS and Stirling would have to fight his own corner. Another problem was Special Operations Executive. SOE had taken note of Stirling's successes and begun to take an interest in the new force. The last thing Stirling wanted was to lose his autonomy by being taken over by them. He also had plans of his own – his new method of warfare needn't just be confined to North Africa, he could see it in use in the European theatre, and he wanted his hands on the steering-wheel as it developed. Already he was working on a more solid identity for the SAS. His men were from different regiments but working as if they were in a new one of their own. Sergeant Bob Tait designed a badge for them: a downward-pointing Excalibur flanked with upward-sweeping flames, crossed with a scroll bearing the words WHO DARES WINS.

Luckily Stirling had Auchinleck's remit and could argue that his brief was to report directly to the C-in-C, but that might only keep SOE at bay for a while. His office at MEHQ was open to eavesdroppers and he had to take every scrap of paper away with him each evening – and Stirling was usually far from fastidious when it came to questions of security.

He decided to move into his brother Peter's flat and use that as his command centre.

The flat was a big, three-bedroomed, two-bathroomed place near the British Embassy, where Peter worked. Plenty of the rather less conventional type of British officer passed through, and the atmosphere was bohemian – the flat served as a dining club, a storeroom, an office, a dormitory, a dead-letter drop, a jumping-off spot for the Gezira Club, the race-course, or Shepheard's; and a place to meet girls. It was presided over by Peter's valet and housekeeper, Mohammed Aboudi. It was important that Mo liked you: once he did, he would be your secretary, manservant, bodyguard and friend. Stirling remembered: 'He was far more efficient than anyone the army could have given me. He was very discreet and I had no hesitation in leaving maps, photographs and notes around the flat. [Stirling gave the impression of being notoriously lax when it came to security.] I only had to tell Mo I wasn't home and no-one would get past the front door. Possibly because his English was limited, he would not take no for an answer on the telephone. If someone hung up on him he would simply re-dial until he got an answer. He was quite happy to liaise directly with anyone in MEHQ: I used him to chase up ammunition, rations, vehicle spares, anything. He was like a terrier – I just used to tell him to use his imagination to get things done, and he did! MEHQ never complained to me. I don't know what they thought and I didn't care. The system worked and I never bothered to explain it to them.'

Meanwhile Stirling had to move fast to get his unit up to strength and once again his adaptability and ability to improvise came to the fore. Hearing of a group of Free French paratroopers lying idle in Alexandria, he went to meet them, persuaded their reluctant General (by invoking the Auld Alliance) that they would be put to good use working with him, and co-opted them, together with their commanders, Georges Bergé and Augustin Jordan. The fact that the men were trained paratroopers was an extra attraction. Despite the failure of the first mission, Stirling didn't want to be entirely dependent on LRDG and continued to have his men parachute-trained.

The raid on Bouerat was set for the night of 23/24 January 1942. The chance of finding tankers in the harbour was slight, as they would arrive, unload and depart in the shortest possible time, but, as his unit was unversed in waterborne attack, Stirling enlisted the aid of the Special Boat Section (which had been involved with Layforce). They brought along with them a collapsible canoe called a folboat (from the German *Faltboot*) – a rubberised canvas shell stretched over a complicated structure of interconnected wooden struts. These craft were hard to assemble and difficult to manage once in the water, but two SBS men were on hand. Nevertheless, the folboat was erected in advance – unluckily, as the truck carrying it hit a pothole on the approach and it was smashed. The approach itself was fraught with danger and setbacks, but at last they found themselves at the target, which was – apparently – unguarded.

As things turned out, the loss of the folboat wasn't as great a setback as it might have been, since there were no oil tankers in the port. However, splitting into two groups, the unit managed to plant bombs on the crates of machinery, supplies and spare parts they found in the huge warehouses near the quays. Then Reg Seekings, who had an uncanny sense of smell when it came to petrol (whose odour he loathed) led them to a large car-park where they discovered ranks of about eighteen petrol tankers lined up. The teams planted more bombs here, before making their way back to the rendezvous point with the LRDG. All bombs had been set to go off as close as possible to 02h00 and the team was well away by the time they had the satisfaction of seeing the sky above Bouerat turn red, and felt the tremor of the explosions reach them through the ground. A third party had gone up the coast to destroy a radio station spotted by air reconnaissance, and they too returned, reporting success.

Stirling was satisfied. He'd shown that his group was effective against targets other than airfields. But in the meantime he'd been out of touch with the course of the war for several days, and in that time the tide had turned. The Afrika Korps had struck back and retaken Benghazi, which had briefly fallen into Allied hands. Rommel had also regained control of western Cyrenaica and had pushed the 8th Army into a defensive position around Gazala.

Bouerat had taught Stirling some useful lessons. News of the military reverse made up his mind to press on immediately with an attack on Benghazi and the German airfields around it. He returned to Kabrit to implement his plans.

Once there he confronted a problem of a different type. He'd left Mayne in charge, and Mayne, unsuited to dealing with administration and bored with training, had gone into a deep depression, and started drinking heavily. Stirling realised that he'd misunderstood the man and underestimated the sense of loss Mayne had felt at the loss of his friend McGonigal. He was only grateful that Mayne had been disciplined enough not to ruffle feathers at MEHQ irreparably – he knew that by now his unit's reputation and Auchinleck's protection would have spared them the worst; but he might well have found himself under the sway of SOE, with his own hands tied. Now, Stirling mended fences fast by involving Mayne in the Benghazi planning – to be met by an immediate change in Mayne's attitude. Together, they set about information-gathering, and Stirling discovered a cache of detailed intelligence information at MEHQ. He enlisted the help of Captain Ken Allot and Lt. David Sutherland of the SBS. He also enlisted Robert Melot, a Belgian resident businessman who was fluent in Arabic and was well-acquainted with the area. Benghazi was a big, busy town, and its port was one of the most important on the coast.

The LRDG had retreated from their former base at Jalo, now in German hands, and relocated to the much more attractive Siwa Oasis. This was to be Stirling's base for the Benghazi operation.

LRDG would continue to look after transport – the 'taxi service' – but Stirling had also acquired his own 'Blitz Buggy'. This was a Ford V8 utility vehicle which he'd managed to 'liberate' in Cairo, and to which he'd made several adaptations. Its engine was fine-tuned; its roof and sides had been removed in order for it to carry a crew of six together with gear and explosives. The boot space now contained an extra petrol canister and the mountings for two Vickers K machine guns – a third Vickers K was mounted on at the front. These could be removed and hidden under the seats – without them, and with the correct paintwork and insignia, the Buggy could pass as a German staff-car. Loaded with a folboat, it would be used in the main raid on Benghazi.

The first outing was abortive because the folboat refused to assemble; but, almost incredibly, the team had penetrated Benghazi without difficulty. For the second attempt Stirling engaged the services of Fitzroy Maclean, a friend and colleague of brother Peter, who had quit the diplomatic service in order to join up and who had very recently completed his SAS training. In Maclean he was to find a formidable and intelligent aide. Furthermore, he spoke fluent and accentless Italian. Maclean obtained two inflatable lightweight dinghies to replace the unreliable folboats. The core of the raiding party, led by Stirling, would be Maclean, two of Stirling's most trusted men, Reg Seekings and Johnny Cooper, and another new arrival – Randolph Churchill. Stirling was sceptical about Churchill's operational ability, but he knew what the value would be of having the Prime Minister's son along on a successful operation. Randolph admired Stirling, and had a natural talent with words, and for PR.

After intense rehearsals, again using a British base as a dummy target, they set off. The Buggy sustained some undercarriage damage on the approach to Benghazi and the engine made a noise 'like a hundred rampant East End tomcats out for a good time', but was otherwise unaffected and despite the noise it was making, they went on. At one point Stirling noticed that Randolph had rum in his water canteen and furiously ordered him to ditch it.

On the outskirts of town they did, at last, attract attention and an Italian army vehicle began to follow them. A car chase into Benghazi followed, and Stirling, driving, as usual, like a maniac, managed to lose his pursuers. Then they heard sirens, though an RAF raid seemed unlikely as Bomber Command was holding off Benghazi while the SAS were operating there. However, it seemed best to get rid of the Buggy, which they hid in a side street. Cooper set a charge in it, timed to explode after thirty minutes. The alarm must have been raised.

The team then set off in the direction of the Arab Quarter. On the way they encountered a Carabinieri officer and Maclean engaged him in conversation. The Italian didn't appear to notice that Maclean and his companions weren't fellow-countrymen, and told them that there might have been an air-raid. Maclean tentatively suggested the possibility of a ground attack, but the Italian laughed that off, telling them that that was out of the question – all the British had scuttled back to Egypt. As soon as Maclean had translated this, the team made their excuses and left, hurrying back to the Buggy to defuse the bomb. Clearly they hadn't been detected after all. The raid was on again.

They made it in time. Randolph was left with Corporal Rose to hide the car close by, and more securely. The others set off with their equipment in search of targets. But then there were more setbacks. The dinghy they'd taken with them refused to inflate – somehow it'd got punctured – so they had to go back to the Buggy to get the other one. But it, too, had been damaged. By now it was almost dawn and they made their way back to the car again, now concealed in a hole in the wall of a bomb-damaged building. The building was deserted and there were rooms above, so they holed up there, despite the fact the '10 Downing Street', as Randolph had dubbed their hideout, was opposite a German Area HQ. Stirling typically took advantage of the daylight to take a stroll down to the harbour dressed in a rollneck and cord slacks – he spoke neither Italian nor German so the risk was great, but at least his recce revealed that there were two patrol boats moored in the harbour which they might be able to destroy that night.

Meanwhile, his comrades worked on the Buggy and fixed the damage it had sustained.

Disappointingly their raid that night was frustrated by its coinciding with a changing of the harbour guard, and they had to withdraw. They couldn't stay any longer as they had to make their rendezvous with LRDG and so they packed up and left, managing at least to destroy a fuel dump on their way out. The Buggy's markings meant that no-one challenged them – Stirling had more than proven by now that security of both Axis and Allied sides was lamentably lax, and perhaps the powers in Benghazi genuinely believed the British were too far away to present any danger on land.

What was of value was the information they had gathered. And Randolph would be sure to make a glowing report to his father.

TEN

David Stirling, throughout his life, was a foolhardy and reckless driver. Soon after the Benghazi raid, driving from Alexandria to Cairo with Churchill, Maclean and Rose on board, he had one of his many car crashes, which left him with a cracked wristbone, but the others with far more serious injuries. Luckily everyone recovered, and Stirling escaped any censure. By now the war in Africa was touch-and-go, Winston Churchill was anxious for positive results, and the SAS needed to push home its strategic usefulness.

Bergé's paratroopers were now officially under Stirling's command (Bergé was in charge of his own French SAS Squadron). Bergé led an expedition to Crete in June 1942, but was betrayed and captured. Meanwhile Augustin Jordan had experienced a similar betrayal in the course of a raid on two airfields at Derna. Complicit in the betrayal was their driver/mechanic, a German ex-Foreign Legionnaire called Brückner, who'd been recruited as an apparently reliable gentile assistant by a small and intrepid unit called Special Interrogation Group.

Meanwhile, also in June, Stirling was launching raids on the airfields of Benina, Berka and Barce. Benina was a major target, and the attack, led by Stirling, was a success, though it was also the occasion of the one act of which David would subsequently be ashamed. He threw a hand-grenade into a crowded German guardhouse with the words, 'Here you are, share this among you!' Later he was to recall: 'It was a silly show of bravado, I suppose. In a fight I would shoot to kill with the same enthusiasm as the next man but I was not at ease with that action. It seemed close to murder.'

In the event, all three actions met with success – but the same could not be said for the Allies, as the fortunes of war continued to favour Rommel. There was, therefore, all the more reason to deploy the SAS to harry the supply-lines of the Germans, which were stretching out further and further as the Afrika Korps thrust eastwards. MEHQ was a little more amenable by now and Stirling was able to requisition a fleet of new jeeps, arm them with Vickers machine guns, and supplement them with a number of supply trucks. Thus he was able to become independent of LRDG. The Blitz Buggy remained Stirling's 'staff car'. The SAS itself now had a core force of 100 battle-hardened men.

By the beginning of July, the force was ready to set out for a prolonged tour of duty in the desert. Much of the terrain was familiar to them by now, and the light jeeps would be able to swoop down on the enemy and then beat a fast retreat in the same manner as, in the past, light infantry or cavalry raiding parties had done. (The Germans never developed a force which specifically mirrored the SAS, though they copied its methods, and Otto Skorzeny of the SS employed its techniques when springing Mussolini from prison on 12 September 1943.)

Operations were subjected to conditions of the strictest secrecy and now the raids were carried out which earned Stirling the 'Phantom Major' nickname Rommel gave him. Although ably supported, Stirling knew he had to remain at the helm and at the centre of every move, both at the front and in his continuing manoeuvrings with MEHQ, and he was pushing himself to the limit.

Nevertheless he had the satisfaction of seeing his brainchild more persuasively vindicated with every day that passed.

This was a double-edged sword. Stirling soon received a summons to Cairo from MEHQ, and there he was apprised of a grand plan in which the SAS was to take part. There was no way at this stage that Stirling was going to put the SAS under anyone else's command, and he responded by emphasising the importance of the SAS' raids on Rommel's airfields and supply lines. MEHQ tried to mollify him by telling him that in any envisaged operation he would have a 'free hand' in SAS deployment.

The plan, the brainchild of Colonel John Haselden, to whom Stirling had unwisely confided earlier about his wider plans for the SAS' future, was for an all-out attack on Benghazi. Haselden was an Arabist and an experienced Intelligence officer, but he had no experience of combat command and Stirling was deeply sceptical about the idea. MEHQ offered him the blandishments of full leadership of the operation, the possibility of expanding the SAS in the wake of a successful attack, and even area command with a free hand. He locked horns with the planners, and in particular with an Air Vice Marshal who, Stirling later learned, had a particular down on him because someone had suggested that as the SAS had accounted for more enemy planes than the RAF, Stirling should be awarded the DFC! Only the diplomatic intervention of an Air Commodore smoothed the waters, and, at the same time, placed Stirling in a position from which he could not refuse the job.

Exhausted, and suffering from the migraines which often plagued him, Stirling retreated to Peter's flat for some much-needed rest and recuperation. But it was not to be. Randolph's glowing PR job on the SAS, based on his participation in the first Benghazi raid, had paid off. His father was in Cairo, and Stirling found himself, together with Fitzroy Maclean, invited to dine with the Prime Minister at the Embassy.

Winston Churchill invited Stirling and Maclean to take a walk with him in the Embassy gardens after dinner, and Stirling used the opportunity to expatiate on his plans for the future of the SAS in operations extending into Italy, and, in his words, 'the soft underbelly of Europe'. Churchill didn't comment much except to ask if he could borrow the phrase as it not only had a good ring to it but accurately described that area of the conflict. In fact, Churchill had been enormously impressed by

Stirling, and that was not shaken by the outcome of the big Benghazi raid, which went ahead and was, as Stirling had feared, a disaster. Only the LRDG raid on Barce airfield as a success, and it had used classic SAS techniques.

Meanwhile the summer passed and lessons were learned. Churchill replaced the hitherto cautious Auchinleck with General Harold Alexander; in the 8th Army, Ritchie was replaced by General Bernard Montgomery. At the same time, MEHQ finally realised the true effectiveness of the SAS, which became a regiment in its own right; David was promoted Lieutenant-Colonel.

But the battle wasn't over. When Stirling approached Montgomery with a request to augment his force by 150 seasoned men in order to continue his successful harrying of Rommel's supply lines, and destruction of his matériel and fuel dumps, he was turned down, Montgomery had a major offensive in mind and had no wish to make any experienced soldiers available to the SAS. It may also have been that Monty needed to demonstrate his authority over Stirling who, in his view, was 'arrogant in the extreme.' For his part, Stirling discovered that the offensive, Operation Lightfoot, was to start on 23 October, and that Allied Landings far to the west in Algiers, Oran and Casablanca – Operation Torch – were scheduled for a fortnight later. If he didn't make the presence of the SAS felt once again before then, his force risked being overlooked and even possibly disbanded. He regrouped his men, formed a squadron ('A' Squadron) under Paddy Mayne's command, and sent them to harass the Matruh railway line. He himself remained at Kabrit to recruit and train a second squadron. He hated staying behind, but he knew he was at the limit of his endurance; and indeed the desert sores (these are infective sores, mainly occurring on the hands and feet, caused by a micro-organism and owing to prolonged desert or veldt walking and exposure), which he'd long been suffering from and ignoring, soon meant another spell in hospital.

Once recovered, good news awaited him. His oldest brother, William, was to raise a second SAS unit in Britain – which rapidly became 2nd SAS Regiment and joined the 1st Army in the west. A full French SAS Regiment was also now in existence. Furthermore, Stirling had the support of General Alexander, and of Monty's General Staff Aide, Colonel John 'Shan' Hackett, with whom Stirling was to hit it off from the first. Stirling then draw up plans whereby 'A' Squadron might be sent to the Lebanon in the near future for terrain training prior to possible deployment in the Middle East and Turkey; and meanwhile his newly-trained men – 'B' Squadron – should join Paddy Mayne and raid the entire length of the German road and rail links between Agheila and Tripoli. 'If we got a move on we ought to be able to coincide with Monty's next offensive, which was planned for December.'

Montgomery was won over and approved the plan. He commented, 'The Boy Stirling is mad. Quite, quite mad. However in war there is often a place for mad people. Now take this scheme of his. Penetrating miles behind the enemy lines. Attacking the coastal road on a 400-mile front. Who but the Boy Stirling could think up such a plan? Yet if it comes off I don't mind saying it could have a really decisive effect on my forthcoming offensive.'

The offensive was successful and the SAS more than played its part in it. Both battles of Alamein had been fought that year and the tide of war had now turned decisively in the Allies' favour. As the 1st Army advanced from the west and the 8th Army from the east, early in 1943 the SAS concentrated their activities on the gap between them, where the enemy was concentrated. Operating in the Gabès Gap, between the

Mediterranean to the east and the Lake Djerid Salt Marsh to the west, Stirling at last fell foul of alert German forces and, with a fellow-soldier, was taken prisoner.

The troops who'd captured him were green, and the two SAS men were able to escape almost immediately – at dusk; but it was not to last. He and the other man – McDermott – became separated during the night and Stirling found himself the following dawn lost and disoriented in the desert. He found a hollow to sleep in, but when he awoke he found a young Arab staring down at him. The youth seemed friendly, and offered food and water, if Stirling would follow him. Stirling really had little alternative, but it came as a shock when the Arab led him straight to an Italian patrol – and this time the men were hardened professionals. The Arab was already sticking a pistol in Stirling's ribs, but David's anger was so great that he dropped down, seized him by his ankles in a lightning movement, and then rose to his feet, whirling the Arab round his head before dashing him to the ground in front of his Italian captors, who quietly raised their weapons.

There was nothing to be done. Stirling was now a prisoner-of-war.

ELEVEN

The SAS was to continue its activities under Paddy Mayne. David had other matters to preoccupy him now.

The worst thing about being a PoW is the inaction, and Stirling felt this, and the loss of liberty, of freedom of choice, more acutely than most. None of his captors yet knew exactly who he was, and he quickly covered the show of fury and extreme strength he'd demonstrated in his treatment of the treacherous Arab by adopting the gentle, bumbling persona which had served him so well in the past. 'At first there was a sort of numbness and a complete refusal to accept the situation. I felt almost insulted. Then I began to feel rather sorry for myself but that didn't last long. I think the main feelings were anger and the most acute frustration imaginable.'

He didn't try to escape at first, but when he was moved from a transit camp to a permanent camp at Gavi early in February, he was rested and recovered, and began to take practical stock of his situation. Gavi was an ancient fortress in Piedmont set on a high hilltop; it looked all but impossible to get out of. Fortunately for Stirling there were several fellow officers there who'd also been taken prisoner, among them Jack Pringle, whom he'd known and liked before the war.

He made the most of it, and even won £100 at roulette the first evening he was there; but Pringle was already involved in an escape plan and soon included him in it. They made their attempt on a cold, wet night in April, 1943, but, though Pringle got away and managed to evade recapture for some time, the rope by which Stirling was descending the outer wall broke, and he had a near-fatal fall.

Italy capitulated to the Allies early in September and the inmates of Gavi – Pringle had unwillingly rejoined them by then – were transported in cattle trucks by the German *Feldpolizei* to Austria. The *Feldpolizei* were brutal and efficient – in contrast to the Italian guards. Nevertheless, another chance of escape presented itself to Stirling and Pringle when the train stopped at Innsbruck, where soldiers of the regular German army took over guard duty. They climbed down from their cattle truck, which wasn't locked, and made off, hoping to reach the Swiss border which was only some 150 kilometres distant. But again their liberty was short-lived.

This time the Germans took a much firmer hand, and they were transferred, via interrogation near Berlin, to Märisch Trübau (Moravská Třebová) in what is now the Czech Republic. Here, David's ability both to organise and command (without ever appearing to dominate) came into its own. He energised his fellow PoWs into planning a mass escape of around 150 men, established an intelligence unit, and even made contact with the local Czech Resistance. Once again Stirling's dilatory attitude to security put them at risk – he would leave papers lying around as soon as he'd absorbed their content – and one of his assistants, Michael Simkins, was all but overwhelmed by the task of clearing up after him – in 1965, Simkins became Director-General of MI5. But there was never any doubting the trust the men under his command put in him – even in a PoW camp. 'He had this extraordinary and almost unaccountable way of convincing you to put your confidence in his ideas, and he did it almost always by suggestion, or implication, never by just telling you outright. He was a perfect combination of Caesar and Cato.'

Daring as the project was, and it was prepared with enormous attention to detail, it was thwarted by the German decision in May, 1944, to transfer the PoWs to a new camp in Braunschweig the following month – June, when the escape was to have taken place. It's almost certain that the Camp Commandant had somehow got wind of the plan. For a moment it looked as if Pringle and Stirling might even face the firing squad. Fortunately, they were spared that, and in Braunschweig Stirling turned his thoughts to the progress of the war – news was constantly filtering in, including information about the German Resistance. This really got Stirling's mind working. If he could contact its members…

But before he could begin to act, there was another transfer. Stirling had established a reputation as a troublemaker, and the Germans had a good idea of who he really was, so now they sent him to a castle about 50 kilometres south-east of Leipzig – *Offizierlager* IV-C – Colditz.

There was no escape, but through guards who'd been friendly for a long time, having been bribed with goodies from Red Cross parcels by the many long-term prisoners, Stirling and Pringle organised and established links with locals, through whom they gathered helpful intelligence. Ultimately they would use this to enable the Senior British Officer, Colonel Willie Tod, to persuade the Commandant, *Oberst* Prawitt, to surrender the castle to them in the face of the inexorable advance of the US Army, and its imminent arrival. Stirling remembered:

'I managed to get down, with our little intelligence cell, to meet the Yanks, and we handed over all the information we had collected, which must have saved them some time. Somehow it seemed like an anti-climax. Soon we were on the move and I think it was 16 April [1945] when we got back to England. I was impatient to see my family and get back to the SAS.'

TWELVE

By then the SAS had grown to five regiments, now under the overall command of Brigadier 'Mad' Mike Calvert – three British, two French, and one Belgian. Accolades for its wartime achievements now poured in from every side, from Eisenhower to Montgomery. Stirling started to plan the future of his creation, but the War Office pre-empted this by deciding to disband it. That decision would later be reversed – the SAS was reformed in October 1947 as part of the Army Air Corps. Stirling had been made First President of the Special Air Service Regimental Association which was founded in October 1945. He was not quite 30 years old. An OBE followed in 1946.

His creation was to grow and flourish, but Sterling was not so lucky. He was one of a breed of men for whom the War provided an opportunity for early glory, and who never quite managed to live up to those achievements. The rest of his life was to provide a coda that was in far more minor key.

That was not for want of trying. He dabbled in African politics and business during the era when the British were retreating from their colonies. At times, he badly needed money and remained a dedicated gambler, most notoriously when a member of the Clermont Club in Mayfair – a high-end casino set up in 1962 by gambler, wildlife enthusiast and zoo owner John Aspinall. Fellow members included Ian Fleming, Lucian Freud, James Goldsmith, Lord Lucan, Kerry Packer and Peter Sellers. Two of Stirling's IOUs amounted to £150,000 and £173,500.

After Africa, television was his next enthusiasm, setting Television International Enterprises Ltd (TIE) from an office in Sloane Street. TIE distributed several early episodes of DR WHO and SESAME STREET, among a host of BBC programmes and series. At its height, it was supplying programmes to twelve independent stations. As many other former SAS men were to do, he also dabbled in private security, creating Watchguard (International) Ltd in 1967, which worked in Libya and across the Middle East. By the early 1970s, Stirling turned his attention to Britain. Holding court at White's, where his practical jokes are still remembered with mixed feelings. At a time of growing industrial unrest, Sterling became convinced of a deeply-laid communist plot, and formed the Greater Britain League. This was perhaps not the happiest choice of name, for the British fascist John Tyndall had formed the (now defunct) Greater Britain Movement in 1964, and Oswald Mosley had written a book entitled THE GREATER BRITAIN in 1932. In his view, the power of the unions would have to be curbed, and an organisation would have to be set up capable of staging a coup d'état if the Government lost control. This organisation, formed from the ranks of the Guards regiments and the membership of White's and similar clubs, became Greater Britain 75 – GB75.

But GB75 never really got off the ground and seems in fact to have been no more than an eccentric last gasp of the Edwardian Establishment. But while he was running it Stirling took it with deadly seriousness, and applied his usual intense concentration to its development, drawing conservative trade unionists and barmy reactionaries alike to his cause, in an unusual alliance. He was convinced of the rightness of what he was doing, and the gravity of what was at stake.

During the 1980s, Stirling began to retreat a little from the ceaseless activity which had characterised his life, dabbling again in Africa, but with waning energy. At the end of his career, he closed down the office in South Audley Street (another expensive address) on grounds of cost; but his career itself was winding down. The years of physical and mental stress, hard-living and hard work, had begun to take their toll on this remarkable giant of a man.

His knighthood came very late in his career – after lobbying by the SAS – and by then he was a sick man. His last public appearance was on 26 October 1990, nine days before his death, at the annual reunion of L Detachment – 'The Originals'.

After the dinner, he returned to the London Clinic, where he was by now resident. His last business venture was to accept the presidency of Saladin Security, but any involvement with it was not to be. Walking down a corridor in the Clinic on Sunday 4 November, he collapsed, to die a few hours later without regaining consciousness, though his sister Margaret, who was with him at his bedside, thought she saw a flash of recognition in his eye in the moment before he left her.

The dramatic rescue of the hostages in the Iranian Embassy siege of 1980 by the SAS has brought the regiment he created to even greater prominence. It became recognized as the template for a new type of warfare: small elite bands of highly trained soldiers who could fight against huge odds. Within a decade, you could hardly turn on the TV or wander into a bookshop without seeing an SAS memoir or thriller. It was probably the best military brand in the world. And yet, its founder was never part of that, and it is unlikely he would have approved. Like the musketeers in the end, David Stirling was a man who had outlived his time. He had made an original, vital, and striking contribution to the war in Africa and, though he had made ethical and moral mistakes in his subsequent career, he had not done so deliberately. He had always steered by his own moral compass and if he was too assertive of his independence and his own rightness of view, that was by nature, not by design. His talent was undeniable, and, properly deployed, it had been invaluable to his country. He would have been happy in that knowledge.

BIBLIOGRAPHY

I am indebted to the writers of the two biographies of David Stirling already in existence:

THE PHANTOM MAJOR by Virginia Cowles (William Collins, 1958)

DAVID STIRLING by Alan Hoe (the authorised biography; Little, Brown, 1992)

and:

SPECIAL AIR SERVICE: MISSIONS DE L'IMPOSSIBLE by Georges Caïtucoli (Presses de la Cité, 2000)

LONG-RANGE DESERT GROUP by W. B. Kennedy Shaw (Collins, 1945)

SAS: THE FIRST SECRET WARS by Tim Jones (Tauris, 2005)

EASTERN APPROACHES by Fitzroy Maclean (Jonathan Cape, 1949)

THE COMPLETE HISTORY OF THE SAS by Nigel McCrery (Carlton, 2007)

STIRLING'S MEN by Gavin Mortimer (Cassell, 2004)

KILLING FOR PLEASURE by Jonathan Rademeyer (Random House Struik, 2012)

DOCUMENTARY:

THE MAYFAIR SET, Episode 1 (Adam Curtis, 1999)

ACKNOWLEDGEMENTS

The following people – among others – have given me either help, suggestions or support. The views expressed in this book should not necessarily be associated with them; and the author takes responsibility for errors.

Marji Campi
Ben Clark
Peter Ewence
Richard Foreman
Lady Raina Haig
Damien Lewis
Matthew Lynn
Jamie Maclean
Christopher Peachment

ANTON GILL
London, January 2015

Printed in Great Britain
by Amazon

11646197R00062